I AM GREATER

KIDS EDITION

GIVE YOUR KIDS PERMISSION TO BE GREAT

BY MARIAH BROWNLEE

Dear Paislee and Hayes,
Never forget that your greater is within you.
Discover it, embrace it, live it.

-Mom

TABLE OF CONTENTS.

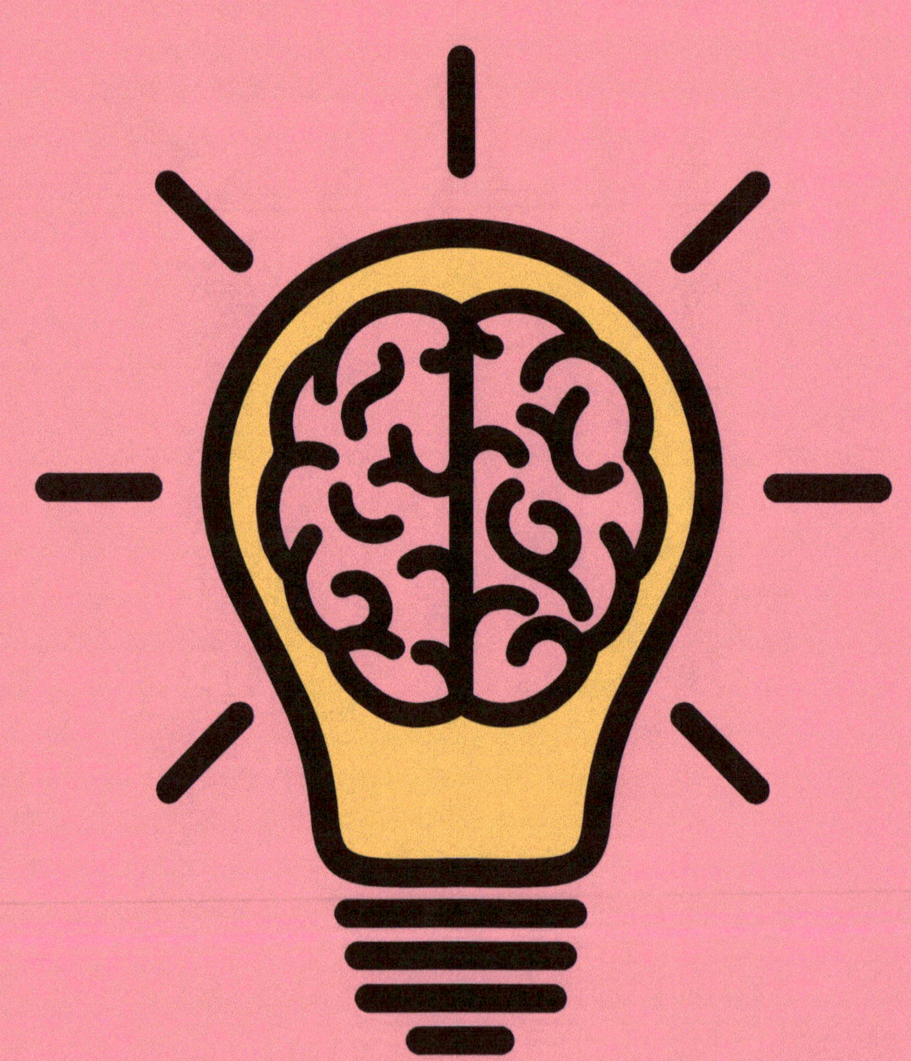

KNOWLEDGE IS POWER.

I am intelligent.
I deserve to learn.
My intelligence can get me anywhere.
My education will make me successful.
My knowledge cannot be
taken away.

2

SHINE BRIGHT.

I am a light.
My light that I bring to the world
cannot be dimmed by anything or anyone.
My light will forever shine bright.

MY PURPOSE IS MY SUPERPOWER.

I have a purpose.
I matter.
My purpose is made special for me.
My purpose matters.

I AM ENOUGH.

Being just enough is not enough.
I am more than enough.
I am worthy.
I am deserving.
I am everything.

DIFFERENT IS GOOD.

There's nobody like me.
I am who I am.
I am unique and that's okay.
I will always be my best self.
Being different is what makes me,
ME!

SELF LOVE
IS IMPORTANT.

I love myself.
I love who I am.
I love how I look.
I love how I talk.
I love every part of me.

12

PERMISSION GRANTED.

I have permission to be great.
I am a leader not a follower.
I can create my own path to success.
I am not afraid of my own greatness.
I am greater.

BE GREAT.